Leader's Guide
for
Your Faith

A Popular Presentation of Catholic Belief

Louis J. Bamonte

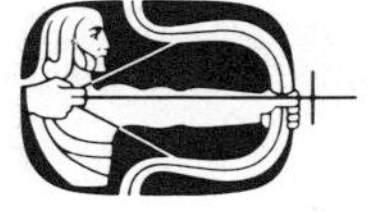

Liguori Publications
One Liguori Drive
Liguori, Mo. 63057

Imprimi Potest:
Edmund T. Langton, C.SS.R.
Provincial, St. Louis Province
Redemptorist Fathers

Imprimatur:
St. Louis, April 28, 1978
+ John N. Wurm, S.T.D., Ph.D.
Vicar General, Archdiocese of St. Louis

ISBN 0-89243-085-0

Printed in U.S.A.
Library of Congress Catalog Card Number: 78-60166

Table of Contents

Welcome to YOUR FAITH!

You are about to travel a road that was first traveled by two disciples of Jesus over two thousand years ago. At the end of his gospel account, Saint Luke picks up the story of the two disciples on the road to Emmaus — men of faith who were discussing all that Jesus had done and said, and all they had experienced as a result of their acquaintance with him. Having accepted the invitation to experience Jesus as a person, they are favored in recognizing Him as Lord. These were indeed special people.

As a successor to these journeyers, you, too, are special. Like your forebearers on the way to Emmaus, you have embarked on a journey of your own — a journey that will hopefully bring you the joy at having experienced the Risen Lord. *Your Faith* and your faith are your companion on this journey.

Your Faith is not a passive companion. It is meant to be conversed with. It will answer some questions and perhaps raise some others. It will challenge and perhaps even change you. It will enable you to turn a corner in your life, believing what J.R.R. Tolkien wrote in *The Fellowship of the Rings:* "Still round the corner there may wait a new road or a secret gate."

Traveling the road to Emmaus, you have accepted an invitation that will enliven the faith that is already yours from Baptism. The road you are on may look different from the one to Emmaus. But if this is so it is not because we have a new doctrine or a new Jesus. It is because it is a new you that is traveling this road — with a belief beyond belief, with a faith refreshed and a faith made personal. This is *Your Faith!*

On the Use of This Guide

This guide presents 15 sessions that correspond to the 15 sections of the book *Your Faith.* Each session has been designed to provide a more than ample amount of material/activities for each section. Thus, *Your Faith* is suitable for a 15-session or a 30-session program.

Although adolescents and adults have different educational needs, the sessions in this guide were designed with both in mind. Thus a certain session might seem to be more adult-oriented than the one that preceeded it. Nonetheless, the flexibility with which this program was designed will insure its successful completion in a group of young people as well.

For the person who is leading or teaching the group, it would be important to read over the material in *Your Faith* prior to reading this Guide. As both are read, the "planner" should ask himself:

What is the essential idea here? How is it to be communicated with the time and resources that I have?

In line with the needs and personality of your group, it is important to keep in mind that creative involvement of all in the learning process is essential. The activities in this guide have been designed to afford maximum involvement of those participating in the program.

All in all, the most significant resource for this program is the group itself — and you with *your faith!*

For an Opening Session

In order to get your group acquainted with one another, and with an overview of the program, distribute copies of the following questions. Allow time for each person to reflect on one or two questions that appeal to him or her.

- ***Can you recall a favorite story from childhood?***
- ***Is there a special story that you enjoy telling?***
- ***Can you recall a funny story about yourself?***
- ***Is there a story from your life that you would really like to be remembered by?***
- ***Can you recall a story of something terrifying that happened to you at one time?***

After those in the group have had time to reflect on these questions (and similar ones that you yourself have offered), ask them what makes for an interesting story. Next, divide the larger group into smaller groups of four to six persons. Ask each person to share one story with the rest of the group.

After all have shared their stories, pose this question:

- ***What would have to be included in a story known as the Christian Story?***

(If time permits, you could have small groups plan out a film script for a film entitled "The Christian Story.")

After you have listed what the group members consider to be the elements of the Christian story, have everyone turn to the table of contents in *Your Faith* and discuss which elements of the Christian story they included and which they left out.

Conclude by asking each person to write a brief statement that answers the question:

- ***What do I expect to happen as a result of this program?***

Section One
Jesus Is the Center of Our Faith
***Your Faith,* pages 2-4**

Synopsis
The person who has accepted the Catholic Faith has accepted the person of Jesus as the center of that faith. It is this faith that invites the believer to ask: Who is Jesus?

Materials Needed
- Paper and pens.
- A copy of the text for each person.

Starting
Divide the group into smaller groups of four to six persons. Each group is responsible for:

(a) selecting a famous person (being careful not to reveal this person's name to any other group);

(b) compiling a list of 10 facts/statements about the person selected;

(c) determining which fact is most revealing of the famous person and labeling it as number 1. This should be done for each fact, labeling as number 10 the least revealing fact.

(d) choosing one person in the group to act as "quiz master."

When all the groups have finished their lists, the quiz master from Group A challenges the other groups to guess his famous person in the following way:

(a) Quiz Master A reveals his Number 10 (least revealing) clue to Group B. If Group B guesses correctly, it gains 10 points; if incorrect, play passes to Group C.

(b) Quiz Master A reveals clue number 9 to Group C and they attempt a guess. If they guess correctly, they receive 9 points; if incorrect, play goes to the next group (or back to group B if there are only three groups).

(c) Quiz Master A continues revealing each clue until the famous person is guessed. The group guessing correctly receives the number of points equal to the clue number.

(d) After Quiz Master A has revealed all his clues, play passes to Quiz Master B, who begins again with step (a).

(e) Play continues until all groups have had their famous person revealed.

Discuss the experience as follows:

- ***Did any one clue give you a better idea of who the person was than all of the rest?***
- ***Does any one clue really give a complete picture? Can any one clue stand alone?***
- ***Do all of the clues taken together really say who that person is?***
- ***What would actually meeting the person add to our description of that person? (It could make that person come alive; be more than a collection of facts.)***

At this point, stress that with all the clues and information about a person, there is no substitute for meeting that person. It is the person himself who gives the "facts" about his life a living quality.

Have the group look at the picture on page 2 of the text, and try the experiment that is described. Check to see if their experience affirms or denies what is said in the book.

Allow time for the rest of page 2 to be read silently. Then discuss:

- ***When looking at the picture on page 2, what was the advantage of looking from far away rather than close up?***
- ***In general, are there both advantages and disadvantages to looking at life from far away and from close up? Are there some things that are better viewed from close up? From far away?***
- ***How does this experiment compare with the famous persons game we played? (To get the best view, we need to view a person as a whole rather than simply look at individual clues.)***
- ***What do both page 2 and the famous persons game tell us about approaching Jesus? (We are meeting a living person and not just compiling a list of facts to be memorized.)***
- ***In terms of the famous persons game, if one were trying to identify the Catholic Church, would the statement "Jesus is the center of the faith" be one of the first or one of the last clues given?***
- ***In terms of the famous persons game, which idea about Jesus would be the least revealing fact? Which idea would be the most revealing fact?***

Sorting

A basic question raised in this section is "Who is Jesus?" Before going any further, it would be important for each person to write a brief essay trying to answer that question. In this essay, significant questions that are relevant to a study of Jesus and the Catholic Faith could also be noted.

Ask the group to read page 3 of the text. As they read they should list or underline the main ideas that are being expressed about Jesus. Discuss:

- ***What pieces of information are mentioned about Jesus?***
- ***How does the information presented compare and contrast with your own profile of Jesus?***
- ***Do you think the historical information given identifies Jesus sufficiently?***
- ***How is Jesus described by Tacitus and Pliny? What is your reaction to these descriptions?***
- ***What is meant by saying that there is no such thing as an impartial observer of the life of Jesus? (The life and message of Jesus demand a response; for some it is positive and for others it is negative.)***

Have the group read "Who Do You Say That I Am?" on page 4 of the text, and then discuss:

- ***What are three ways of looking at the person of Jesus?***
- ***Which way comes closest to your own experience of who Jesus is? Are there other alternatives not mentioned in the book?***
- ***In what way are the three descriptions given on page 4 both valid and invalid descriptions of Jesus?***
- ***How do these descriptions differ from a Christian's belief in Jesus? (The Christian is a person who believes that Jesus makes a basic difference in his life. He is a follower of Jesus. He believes that Jesus rose from the dead and still lives.)***
- ***What is being expressed in the diagram on page 4, second column?***
- ***How do these viewpoints on Jesus agree or disagree with your own reflections?***

Summary

Divide the class into the groups that were used at the start of this session. Ask each group to imagine that they have selected Jesus as their famous person and to repeat the process of listing facts and determining which facts are most revealing. Have each group present its list and then discuss:

- ***How well do these ideas answer the question: "Who is Jesus?"***
- ***If the statement "You are the Christ, the Son of the Living God" were to appear on your list, would it be considered a number 10 (least revealing statement) or a number 1 (most revealing statement)? Why?***
- ***Is Peter's declaration the best description of Jesus for one who believes? Why?***

Section Two
Background to the Life of Jesus
Your Faith, pages 5-8

Synopsis

To see the significance of the words "you are the Christ" is to understand the religious and social background of Jesus.

Starting

Present the following list of TV characters to your group: Fonzie, Richie Cunningham, Shirley Feeney, Laverne DeFazio, Jim-Bob Walton, Vinnie Barbarino, Arnold Horshack, Rhoda Morgenstern, Chuck Barris, Johnny Carson, Susan Alexander, Hawkeye Pierce, Jim Rockford, Joe Peters, Jody Campbell, David Bradford. (Add other names to this list in accord with TV programing in your area.) Ask the students to select the character that would best complete the following statements for them:

- ***I would really get in a knock-down, drag-out fight if anyone ever said I was like ____________________________________.***
- ***It would bother me, but I wouldn't get violent, if someone said I was a lot like ____________________________________.***
- ***I'd really like it if someone said I was a lot like ____________.***

Discuss what it would mean to be called a "Fonzie" or a "Chuck Barris" and take a poll on the characters that people in your group would find particularly bothersome. When you get to the names Joe Peters and Susan Alexander, you'll find that not too many people would be bothered or insulted by these names because neither Joe's nor Susan's background is known. Discuss:

- ***Why might you be insulted if someone called you an "Arnold Horshack"? (Because the character of Arnold, on the TV show "Welcome Back, Kotter," is known to all.)***
- ***Why do you think not too many people were bothered by being called a Susan Alexander or a Joe Peters? (Both of these characters have no background established for them.)***

- ***What do you think was the point of this activity? (It is important to know the background of a situation before a person can make a judgment about that situation.)***
- ***Suppose this same list of characters were to be presented to a group for the same activity 500 years from now. Do you think there would be any difference in their reaction?***

To further establish the importance of knowing the background of a situation, have people in the group brainstorm what they would consider to be controversial headlines, such as "Haldeman Calls Nixon the Watergate Master-Planner." Perhaps having some newspapers available would be of help.

When the list is completed add this headline from the *Jerusalem Times:* "Peter Calls Jesus of Nazareth 'the Christ.' " Then have the group rank all of the headlines from the most explosive to least explosive. Discuss their rankings and then ask:

- ***Why was Peter's headline ranked as it was? What is there about this statement that could make it one of the most explosive headlines in the list?***

Sorting

Explain that to know the meaning of Peter's words "You are the Christ," it is necessary to know where and how Jesus lived. It is possible that the more we know about the life and times of Jesus, the more explosive these words become.

Have the group read the bottom of page 5 of the text. Discuss:

- ***Did the fact that Jesus came from Nazareth affect how he may have been viewed by others?***
- ***Are there places in the world today that could be considered a Nazareth?***

Ask the group to read page 6 and study the diagram carefully. Stress that architecture is one of the most permanent expressions of an individual or society. Discuss:

- ***What values do you find expressed in the diagram of the synagogue interior?***
- ***What activities took place in the synagogue? (The dreams and hopes of the Israelite nation were taught and discussed.)***
- ***How does the activity of the synagogue make the words "You are the Christ" more significant?***

- ***Why do religious groups so often restrict activities to a particular age or sex group? Do these restrictions happen anywhere today?***

Ask the group to read "The Temple" on pages 6-7 of the text. Discuss:

- ***What do nerve centers reveal about the people who maintain them?***
- ***Even though the Temple in Jerusalem was the nerve center for the Israelites, what was the one thing that kept them together as a community?***
- ***What was the importance of the Temple and the Holy of Holies?***
- ***Why would Jesus' calling himself "the Temple" provoke controversy? (Because he was identifying himself with the very nerve center of their lives.)***
- ***What event was Temple worship based upon?***
- ***What was the importance of celebrating the Passover and other festivals?***
- ***How does the celebration of these events add to the significance of the words "You are the Christ"? (The dreams and hopes of the awaited Messiah were also recalled in this celebration; it was the thing that kept the Israelites from despair.)***

For a discussion of the social background to Peter's declaration, have the group read page 8 of the text. Then discuss:

- ***What did each group – Zealots, Essenes, Pharisees – believe about the coming of the Christ? What was the one thing they all had in common?***
- ***How did Jesus' life show a reversal of all that the Zealots, Essenes, and Pharisees believed about the Christ?***

Summary

Have the group read "The Question" on page 8 of the text. Ask them to imagine that they overhear Peter say "You are the Christ." With all that they know and have experienced with respect to Nazareth, the synagogue, the Temple, and the celebration of Exodus, what would their feelings be at this moment? Would these words by Peter be explosive words?

- ***Did you ever feel that "Christ" was simply Jesus' last name?***

- ***As a result of this session, have these words become more explosive for you?***
- ***When Peter spoke these words, was he speaking for the entire Jewish nation?***
- ***What had Peter been able to do that others had not done?***
- ***How is making a personal discovery of Jesus different from simply knowing about Jesus? (A personal discovery of Jesus means that he still lives for me and makes a difference in my life.)***

At this point, it would be good for those in your group to reread the essay they wrote in the first session on "Who is Jesus?" After they have reread their essays, ask them to decide whether their answer is more of a personal discovery of Jesus, or a collection of facts about him.

Section Three
Jesus Revealed God to Man
***Your Faith,* pages 9-12**

Synopsis

Jesus spoke of himself as the One who reveals the Father — who is the Way, the Truth and the Life.

Materials Needed

- Paper and pen for each person.

Starting

Ask everyone in the group to list on a piece of paper 10 "I AM" statements that each person feels describe himself or herself in some way. After this has been done, have those that wish to share different ideas that they wrote. Discuss the different ways in which a person might describe himself. Ask:

- ***Did anyone describe themselves in terms of ideas presented at the top of page 9? Are these ideas an adequate representation of the identity of a person?***
- ***Did anyone describe themselves in terms of a symbol – for example, "I am a cool breeze on a hot summer day"?***

At this point have each person add three symbol-like descriptions to their list, then discuss:

- ***Which way of describing yourself do you think says more – the factual material or the symbolic material? Why?***
- ***In terms of symbols, how do you think Jesus would describe himself?***
- ***In terms of facts, how do you think Jesus would describe himself?***
- ***According to page 9, what images did Jesus use to describe himself?***

At this time discuss the various meanings of the symbol-images used by Jesus that are mentioned on page 9 of the text (bread of life, resurrection, etc.)

Sorting

In addition to using these symbols, Jesus also described himself as the Way, the Truth and the Life. Before asking your group to read these sections on pages 10-11 of the text, have each person make three columns on a piece of paper. At the top of the first column, write the word *Way;* at the top of the second column, the word *Truth;* at the top of the third column, the word *Life.* Under each word they should jot down other words and ideas that come to their minds when they think of the word at the top of each of these columns. These will be used as you discuss the material on pages 10-11 of the text.

Ask the group to read "Jesus is the Way" on page 10 of the text, and then discuss:

- ***What word associations did you make for the word* Way?**
- ***If someone said to you, this is the way, what would they be telling you?***
- ***What does it mean to say that Jesus is the Way?***
- ***Was Jesus as a Way to God different from the Old Testament concept of a way to God?***
- ***What did Jesus teach us about sonship in the kingdom of God?***

Ask the group to read "Jesus is the Truth" on pages 10-11 of the text, and then discuss:

- ***What word associations did you make for the word* Truth?**
- ***If someone said to you, "I'm telling you the whole truth," what would they be saying?***
- ***What does it mean to say Jesus is the Truth? (He not only reveals the whole truth about God but he* is *the whole truth about God – "He who sees me, sees the Father.")***
- ***If Jesus gives us the whole picture of God the Father, what can we say about the Father from Jesus' life on earth?*** (This question could be discussed in small groups and then shared in the larger group.)

Ask the group to read "Jesus is the Life" on pages 10-11 of the text and then discuss:

- ***What word associations did you make for the word* Life?**
- ***If someone were to say to you, "This is the life," what would they be saying to you?***

- ***What is your idea of the best possible life for yourself?***
- ***What is meant by the saying,* Jesus is the Life?**
- ***How is doing something about life coming to terms with death?***
- ***Would accepting Jesus as the Life demand something of a transformation in our present lives?***
- ***What are some life-giving ideas of Jesus?***

Before reading the section "God and Ourselves" on page 12 of the text, discuss with your group the meaning of the word Trinity. Then ask them to read this section on page 12. Discuss:

- ***Why haven't the teachings on the Trinity made more of a difference in the lives of people in the past?***
- ***What ideas are brought out in this section that could make this doctrine more meaningful?***
- ***What has Jesus revealed about the Trinity?***

In anthropomorphic terms, the following questions might be of use in helping the group discuss their view of God:

- ***Using human years, how old do you think God would be?***
- ***How do you think God would dress today?***
- ***Is God's attitude toward you mostly critical or accepting?***
- ***Is God actively or passively involved in the lives of people today?***
- ***If God were to speak to you today, what would be the tone of his voice?***
- ***If God had a night free, how would he spend his time?***
- ***If God had a choice, would he prefer to be at home or go out?***
- ***If you had something to discuss with God, would you have to make an appointment with him?***
- ***Would you go to God or would he come to you?***
- ***Would you meet him at his office or in a park?***

Summary

To allow those in your group to reflect a little more deeply on the images of Jesus and God the Father presented in this section, divide the group into smaller groups of four to six. Ask each group to select one image for God or Jesus from this section — for example, Jesus is the Truth — and then to recycle it into a title for a soon-to-be-released motion picture. After this has been done, each group should prepare a one-minute advertising (TV or radio) spot for this new film. These could then be shared and discussed.

Section Four
Jesus Is Our Redeemer
***Your Faith,* pages 13-16**

Synopsis

In a world that is experiencing the results of being lost and disconnected from God, Jesus is here to reestablish the relationship that once existed between God and man.

Materials Needed

- A phonograph.
- Recordings: "Eight Days a Week"; "She's Leaving Home"; "Imagine."
- Optional: printed lyrics of the three songs for each person.

Starting

Present the following situation to your group:

- ***Imagine you are living in the year 3000 A.D. and in going through the national archives you come across three songs that are dated sometime around 1970. Listen to the three songs and write down what you would conclude about life in that era.***

At this point play the three songs ("Eight Days a Week," "She's Leaving Home," and "Imagine" — other songs could also be used), pausing between each one to allow time for those in the group to jot down their ideas about the kind of world being described in each song. If possible, it would also be good to have copies of the words to each song available. Discuss:

- ***What kind of world is being described in the song "Eight Days a Week"? (It is a world where family life seems to flourish; a happy world; a world where love prevails.)***
- ***What kind of world is being described by the song "She's Leaving Home"? (It is a world where there are broken families, lack of communication and lack of love.)***
- ***What kind of world is being described by the song "Imagine"? (It is a world that has been lost, but has hope of being found again.)***

- ***As a person living in the year 3000 A.D., what could you conclude about the world in which these songs were written? (It was a world that contained a mixture of happiness and sorrow; of love and hate; of communication and loneliness.)***

Ask the group to read pages 13 and 14 of the text. Then discuss:

- ***Does the world view presented by the songs agree with what is presented in the book?***
- ***What is your reaction to what is presented in the book?***
- ***Do you feel that man is in need of redemption? Do you feel all that man has done is in need of redemption?***

Sorting

Ask the group to read "Why did Jesus Come?" on page 14 of the text. Explain that there was a time when God and man shared a perfect relationship similar to the one described in the song "Eight Days a Week"; evil entered the world and it became a "She's Leaving Home" type of world — lost and apart from God. Discuss:

- ***Is that where God left the world? (No, the world described by the song "Imagine" is the world in which we recognize that we've been lost, but we don't have to stay lost.)***
- ***How is sin described in this part of the book?***
- ***If sin is described in terms of being lost, list as many of these "lost" experiences as you can.***
- ***How is it possible to be found and in touch with God again? (Through Jesus.)***

Before reading "A Shattering Truth" on pages 14-15 of the text, ask:

- ***Whose fault is it that man is lost – God's, or man's, or is there some other reason?***

After this has been discussed have the group read this section and discuss:

- ***According to this section, whose fault is it that man is lost?***
- ***Who takes the first step in restoring the relationship?***
- ***What is the power of the words "I have come to seek out and save what was lost"?***
- ***What is the power of the selection about the Good Shepherd on pages 14-15? Is it possible to recycle the image of shepherd into a***

more contemporary image that would convey the same idea?

- ***What are the conditions that God sets down in order that we be redeemed? (None. It's a no-strings-attached type of proposition in which we must only want to be redeemed and accept God's love.)***
- ***How does this differ from other religions and philosophies?***

Before reading the section "What did Jesus do for us?" present this story to your group:

- ***One day, Pelé, the great soccer player, saw some children in a ghetto playing with trash in an empty lot. He decided to begin a summer camp for these children and took 30 of them to a place he had bought in the foothills of the Pocono Mountains, in Pennsylvania. There, he taught them everything he knew about being a soccer player as well as what it means to live as a person in the world today.***

Ask the students to read "What did Jesus do for us?" on page 15 of the text and then discuss:

- ***What can we say of both Pelé and Jesus? (Both shared a free gift. Both lived among the people they served. Both tried to show a positive side of man. Both were an example for others to follow. Both made it possible for others to live a better life.)***
- ***In what way are Pelé and Jesus different? (Although Pelé may have had an influence on one group of people, Jesus made it possible for the entire world to overcome the power of sin and evil.)***
- ***How did Jesus make it possible for man to overcome the power of sin and evil? (Through his death and Resurrection.)***

Point out the "mystery" quality of this statement and ask the group to read "Why did Jesus die on the cross?" on page 15 of the text.

- ***Why did God send Jesus?***
- ***Why did Jesus suffer?***
- ***What does Jesus' experience with suffering tell us about our own suffering?***

Continue reading on page 16 and then discuss:

- ***Is the Resurrection a mere proof that Jesus was truly God?***

- ***As close as we can come to it, what is the meaning and value of the Resurrection of Jesus for us?***
- ***If we have been redeemed, why are there still wars and people hurting each other?***
- ***When does salvation come to each of us?***
- ***What is the important connection between the death and Resurrection of Jesus and the celebration of the Eucharist?***

Summary

The book points out that salvation has already begun and yet has not yet been completed. Ask your group to reflect and discuss the following two questions:

- ***What are the signs in the world today that salvation has already begun? How would you go about "proving" this to someone else?***
- ***What are the signs in the world today that salvation has not yet been completed?***

Section Five
Jesus Sends the Holy Spirit
Your Faith, pages 17-20

Synopsis

The Holy Spirit is the life-giving, truth-giving community-building presence in the Church today.

Materials Needed

- A copy of the New American Bible.

Starting

This section and the next deal with two complementary aspects of the Church. Section Five speaks of the essence of the Church — the fellowship of the Holy Spirit as the One who makes the Church what it is: *one people.* Section Six is concerned more with structural elements within the Church. Both sections are introduced with reference to the following fantasy experience. (Before you begin it is necessary to inform your group of what you will be doing. First ask them to find as comfortable a place as possible. If there is a rug on the floor, you might suggest that they sit or lie on the floor. Next, ask them to close their eyes and relax their bodies as much as they possibly can. It is essential that the room be totally still and silent.) Slowly read the following passage to the class, pausing where suggested (/):

- ***Let your mind relax/empty it as much as you can/picture yourself on an island in the middle of an ocean/you've been stranded on this island for several days/ as you stand on the beach, you are looking around/ take note of all you can see/ listen to all the sounds and identify as many individual ones as you can/ take some deep breaths and experience any smells that you can/walk around a bit/you see something about 100 yards away/what does it look like from afar/ run toward it and touch it/ how does it feel/ you see some other people/ how do they look/ speak to them/ what are you speaking about/ stay with them for awhile and then move away and be by yourself again/as you gaze into the ocean, you are wondering about your experience on this island/how are***

you feeling/ stay with your feelings for awhile/ as I count backward from five you can gradually open your eyes.

When everyone is ready, form groups of six to eight people and have the members of each group share what they experienced in their island fantasy. Once this has been done, each small group should discuss and put the following information on a large piece of poster paper or newsprint:

(a) What are the things that could be life-supporting or life-giving for your group on this island?

(b) What do you need in order to keep together as a community on this island?

(c) What do you need in terms of material survival?

(d) What is your source of vitality and strength as a group?

(e) what could you do to keep yourselves amused?

(f) If you were to compare your island to another, what would make yours special and unique?

When all groups have finished, gather everyone into the larger group and discuss the experience as follows:

- ***Did anyone think of the word* spirit *in all of this?***
- ***Is there any importance to it in this situation? What would be its function?***

Have those in the group read page 17 in the text and then ask:

- ***What is the function of the Spirit in the Church according to this part in the book?***
- ***Are there any connections to be made between your island fantasy and the Spirit in the Church?***
- ***Does any statement contained in this part of the book express your experience of Church?***

Sorting

Ask the group to read pages 18-19 and list or underline any connections they see between the island fantasy experience and the experience of the Spirit in the Church. A chart comparing the two experiences could be constructed by the entire group and then a discussion could be held using the following questions:

- ***What important doctrine has been neglected among Christians? Why?***

- ***What was the function of the Spirit of God in the Old Testament?***
- ***How was the Spirit a source of life? Can any comparison be made here to the source of life on your island?***
- ***What is the function of the Spirit in the New Testament?***
- ***What is the function of the Spirit in the early Church?***
- ***Was it easier for the apostles to believe all that Jesus had revealed than it is for us today? Why or why not?***

Have the group read the top half of page 20 in the text and then discuss:

- ***According to the passage from John, what is the function of the Spirit in our lives?***
- ***What does it mean to be a witness?***

Have the group read the last section on page 20 of the text, "The Church is Holy," and discuss the following:

- ***Why does the Church receive criticism in our own time?***
- ***Would you criticize the Church along the same lines?***
- ***Is it a contradiction to say that the Church is holy even when it sometimes appears not to look so holy?***
- ***What is meant by the holiness of the Church?***
- ***What did Jesus teach about holiness?***
- ***If people in the Church were to allow the Spirit to make them holy, what would be the effect?***

Summary

Have someone read Acts 2:1-21 from the New American Bible. After it has been read, ask the following:

- ***How does this passage make you feel? What are some of the stronger feeling words in the passage?***
- ***How is the Spirit described in this passage?***
- ***Does this passage seem to make you more excited or less excited about the role of the Spirit in your own life?***

Section Six
The Church Makes Jesus Present Today

Your Faith, pages 21-24

Synopsis

The Church of Jesus Christ has a structure that enables it to be of service to the People of God.

Materials Needed

- Optional: paper and colored pens for drawing.
- A supply of colored pipe cleaners.

Starting

Have your group assume the smaller groups which they had in the last session and express (in words, in a skit, or in a drawing) what it was like to be on the island. Ask each group to share their work and then ask everyone to read page 21 of the text. Discuss the connections between their experience of trying to express their island experience and trying to describe the Church.

Resume island groups and add this piece of information:

- ***You have been on the island for several months and there seems to be no hope of rescue.***

Each group should now consider themselves a separate island. They should discuss and list on a piece of newsprint their conclusions to the points below. (Members of each group could work in pairs to do different parts of this experience. However, if time is not a factor for you, it would be better not to suggest this; simply let it happen. Later you could also discuss the process of how the group organized itself as well as the conclusions they reached.) The points to be discussed are:

(a) Give a name and a brief biography of the island — what it looks like; advantages; disadvantages; geographical survey, etc.

(b) List the three problems and conflicts you will face personally and as a group, and give possible creative solutions for each.

(c) Determine the type of government, if any, that would be suitable and how it would be set up. Determine what kind of leadership is needed.

(d) Identify different groups of people on the island and their functions and talents.

(e) Determine the values this community intends to live by (traditions) and the values they intend to pass on to future generations. Also tell how they intend to pass on these values.

When all groups have finished, share and discuss the results of their efforts. In a general way, have the group read through the rest of this section (pages 22-24 in the text) and note the similarities between their experience and the experience of establishing the Church. The differences between the two experiences could also be noted. It should also be pointed out that the group experience in this session differed from the one in the last session. In Section Five, a key question was: "What makes the Church, the Church?" In this section the question became: "What is the best way to insure that the Church always remains what it was intended to be by Jesus?"

Sorting

The book divides the establishment of the Church into three time periods: the time before Jesus; the time of Jesus; and the time of the early Christian community. Have the group read page 22 and discuss:

- ***What happens to people who claim to have a special position among others?***
- ***How was this true in the case of the Jews? the early Christians? people today?***
- ***Where does the Catholic Church have its origins?***
- ***What leaders were involved in the formation of the People of God before the time of Jesus?***
- ***What happened to the Old Testament and its message when Jesus arrived? (He came not to destroy but to fulfill. Perhaps it would be beneficial to brainstorm words that mean the same as the word fulfill.)***

Have the group read the section "Jesus chooses his apostles" on pages 22-23 of the text, and ask:

- ***What does the word* apostle *mean?***

- ***How else are apostles described in this section?***
- ***Why is the number 12 so significant?***

Have the group read "Peter: Leader of the Apostles" on page 23 of the text, and discuss:

- ***Was Peter really needed as a leader for the apostles?***
- ***What qualities did Peter possess?***
- ***Why do you think the "rock" image was used?***
- ***Are you comfortable with the "rock" image for a leader in the Church? If not, what image would you prefer?***
- ***What important function did Peter serve in the early Christian community?***

Have the group read "The Command to Serve" on page 23 of the text and discuss:

- ***According to what you have read, what is the function of authority in the Church established by Jesus?***
- ***Was service a value of your island community?***
- ***What image did Jesus use to illustrate what he meant by service?***
- ***In contemporary terms, whose "feet need washing" today?***

The book next discusses the structure and organization of the Church today. It is important to point out that the present-day structure derives its strength and concept from what has been discussed in this section thus far. Have the group read "Organization of the Church" on page 23 of the text and then discuss:

- ***What is the key to a true understanding of the organization of the Catholic Church?***
- ***What does it mean to say that the authority of those in the Church must be Christlike?***
- ***To what extent is the organization of the Church still based on the command to serve?***

Have the group read about the present structure of the Church on pages 23-24 of the text. Before discussing this section, divide into four smaller groups. Give each group a supply of colored pipe cleaners. Instruct two groups to use the pipe cleaners to diagram the Church as it is presented in the book. Instruct the other two groups to use the pipe cleaners to construct a diagram of the Church as they would like to see it. In order for each group to do this, they will need to shape each pipe cleaner into symbols for Pope, bishops, and so on, and then lay them out in a pattern. When both sets of groups have finished, have them make comparisons between the four ways of looking at the structure of the Church. Then discuss:

- ***What is your reaction to the way the book presents the structure of the Church?***
- ***How does the structure of the Church as presented in the book relate to the structure you established for your island community?***
- ***If there could be only one group in the Church, which group would be most essential to retain?***

Summary

Have the group read the section "A Sign to the World" on page 24 of the text. Discuss:

- ***What is the most important reason for the existence of the Church?***
- ***What are some ways in which we make Jesus present to each other and to those who are not members of the Church?***
- ***What other values do Church members seek to pass on to future generations? How do these compare with the values that were listed in the island fantasy experience?***

Section Seven
The New Testament
Your Faith, pages 25-28

Synopsis

It is the function of the Church to pass on and keep alive the presence and the message of Jesus. The Church does this through the New Testament.

Materials Needed

- Paper and pens.

Starting

An essential idea in this section is that the message of Jesus is a message for all men in every age. To involve the group in this thought, have everyone think about and describe what happens in a typical "morning-after" type of commercial. (A man wakes up and complains that his life is a mess and that he has a bad headache. The announcer's voice is heard, suggesting the sure remedy and giving three reasons why this product is the best. The man tries the remedy and is living proof that the product works.)

Divide the group into four smaller groups of six to eight people. Each smaller group is a group of commercial producers working in one of the following time periods of history: (a) 70 A.D.; (b) the Middle Ages; (c) 1776; (d) the present. First, have each group list all the problems that could make a person's life a mess at their moment in history. Then have them write their script for the commercial, suggesting that the remedy is the New Testament and convincing the person in the commercial why this is so by giving three reasons why the New Testament is really the answer to his problems.

After each group has written and presented its commerical, have everyone read page 25 of the text. Then discuss as follows:

- ***What were the different problems mentioned in each commercial? What does this suggest about history?***
- ***Did the solution or remedy in each commercial seem to fit despite circumstances that may have changed? What does this suggest about the message of Jesus?***

- ***Is it true to say that the apostles had a more complete and fuller experience of the message of Jesus than we do?***
- ***Where do we experience the message of Jesus today?***

Before going on, have the group look at the words "Jesus Still Speaks . . ." at the bottom of page 25 in the text. Have each person register a "yes," or a "yes with reservations," or a "no" in the book next to the words "Jesus still speaks . . ." and write a reason why they feel this way.

Sorting

Before reading the next section, construct a "things to do" type of list that may have been done in 70 A.D. by the apostles. Have the group read "Understanding the New Testament" and compare their "Things to Do" list with what the apostles actually did. Discuss:

- ***What is the first step in understanding the New Testament?***
- ***Where does the value of the "written and spoken Word" originate?***
- ***What was read by the early Christians at their worship services?***
- ***What are the reasons that the message of Jesus was not written down immediately after he died and rose?***
- ***What finally gave a push to the writing down of the message of Jesus and the preachings of the apostles?***

Have the group read "How the Gospels were formed" on page 26 of the text and then discuss the three stages in the development of The Gospel as we have it today. The next section "What is a Gospel?" should be preceded by a discussion of the answer that people in your group would give to someone who asked them that question.

Discuss:

- ***What is the order of the stages in the formation of the Gospels?***
- ***What becomes evident from examining the stages of Gospel formation?***
- ***In what way would you say the New Testament is like an ordinary book? In what way is it different?***
- ***Why is "history book" an inaccurate phrase for describing the Gospel?***
- ***Why is biography an inadequate way of describing the Gospel?***

- ***How does John describe the Gospel?***
- ***What are two ways of telling a story? Applying this to the Gospel, which way of telling a story is more in line with what we have in the Gospel?***
- ***What are the characteristics of a portrait? of a photograph? Which do you think is more typical of the Gospel?***
- ***What is the "answer" given to the question "What is a Gospel?"***

To put your group in touch with the content of each of the four Gospel accounts, have everyone read the section entitled "The four Gospels" on pages 26-27 of the text. Then divide the group into four smaller groups. Assign each group a different Gospel. The members of each group first reread the description of their assigned Gospel found on pages 26-27 in the text, and then look through a copy of the New Testament to find five pieces of evidence that support what the book asserts about that particular Gospel. When each group has completed its work, the results can be shared.

Have those in your group read "The Canon of Scripture" on page 28 of the text, and then discuss:

- ***How many books are there in the New Testament?***
- ***Were these books gathered together at random?***
- ***What is meant by the "Canon" of Scripture?***
- ***What factor determines if a particular piece of writing belongs in the Canon of Scripture?***

Have your group read "The Church's Book" at the bottom of page 28 in the text and then discuss:

- ***How does the Bible bring the past into the present?***
- ***What is meant by saying that the Word of God is alive and active?***
- ***What is meant by saying that the Word of God is a double-edged sword?***
- ***What does it mean to read the Scriptures in context?***

Have your group read "St. Paul's Letters" on page 28 of the text and discuss:

- ***What kind of writing is contained in the writings of St. Paul?***
- ***What is the difference between Paul's letters and the material we find in the Gospel accounts of Matthew, Mark, Luke, and John?***
- ***For what reasons did Paul write his letters?***

Summary

Based upon what has been discussed in this section, have the students, in groups or individually, write a book review of the New Testament, expressing their recommendation or non-recommendation of this book for wide readership.

Section Eight
The Sacraments — Baptism
Your Faith, pages 29-32

Synopsis

The sacraments are visible signs of God's love. Baptism is the sacrament by which we begin a new life in Jesus by being freed from sin and initiated into the Church.

Materials Needed

- Paper and pens.

Starting

Divide the group into six smaller groups. Each group is given one of three questions:

(a) What is love?
(b) What is happiness?
(c) What is peace?

Each of the three questions is answered by two groups. One of the two groups that has question (a) may answer the question by using words only. The other group may only demonstrate an answer to the question (by means of a skit). The same thing applies to questions (b) and (c).

After each group has discussed and planned its task, the answers are presented and discussed according to which answers seemed most effective — the ones with words or the ones that were demonstrated.

After the small groups have answered the questions, have the whole group read page 29 in the text and then discuss:

- ***Which statements about man do you agree with? Which do you disagree with?***
- ***Does our experience above prove or disprove that it is easier to understand concrete ideas rather than abstract ideas? What does your own experience say to you about this?***
- ***When God decided to save what was lost and tell man that he was special, what method did he use?***
- ***What was God's concrete sign to man of his love?***

Sorting

Have the group read the first column on page 30 of the text and then discuss:

- ***Why is the birth of Jesus no ordinary sign?***
- ***How is Jesus' birth more than a sign of God's love?***
- ***What is the significance of the Christmas story for the believing Christian?***
- ***What has Jesus himself established in order to insure that God's love will be remembered and celebrated?***
- ***In what way is each of the sacraments a sign of God's love?***
- ***Are the seven sacraments the only sacraments that are available to man? (No, actually anything that enables us to experience the love of God can be considered a sacrament in a general sense.)***
- ***What are some examples of these sacraments (sacraments in the broad sense of the word)?***

Very often, a person's attitude toward sacramental celebration has been affected by past experience with these celebrations. Perhaps this would be a good opportunity to allow the people in your group to explore their attitudes. You could do this by presenting the following pairs of words and phrases and asking them to register which position is closest to their own.

Sacraments are:

- ***a waste of time/ time well spent.***
- ***meaningless routines/ meaningful acts.***
- ***not related to my life/ helpful in my life.***
- ***boring and uninteresting/ truly celebrations.***
- ***producing no change in my life/ making a difference in my life.***
- ***mere words/ real prayer.***
- ***things I do because I have to/ things I do because I want to.***

The text now turns its attention to a discussion of the sacraments in this and subsequent sessions. Have the group read "Baptism" on page 30 of the text and discuss their reaction to the situation presented. Discuss:

- ***According to this teaching about Baptism, what are the three effects of the sacrament of Baptism?***

Have the group read "Entry Into the Church" on pages 30-31 of the text and discuss:

- ***What does it mean to say that we have become more community-conscious in recent years?***
- ***List some evidence that supports the idea that we have become more community-conscious.***
- ***Is it accurate to say that the sacrament of Baptism is a community-conscious sacrament?***
- ***Who is at the center of Christian community?***
- ***How is Christian community different from community established elsewhere?***
- ***What image does St. Paul use to describe Christian community? Can you think of other images that might also apply?***
- ***If you were planning the Baptism of someone you knew, what would you plan into the celebration so that the idea of entry into the Church would be stressed?***

Have the group read "New Life in Christ" and "Power to Worship" on page 31 of the text, and then discuss:

- ***What does the word* Baptism *mean? What does it have to do with the death and Resurrection of Jesus?***
- ***How was Baptism performed in the early Christian community?***
- ***What does it mean to say that Baptism is more of a burial than a washing?***
- ***How did the early Christian community stress the importance of Baptism as the first sacrament?***
- ***What does it mean to have the power to worship?***

Have the group read "Freedom From Sin" on page 31 of the text and discuss:

- ***What are some things that you would like to be free from?***
- ***What freedom does Baptism give us?***
- ***What quality of Jesus is brought out in the sacrament of Baptism?***
- ***As baptized Christians, are we called to live out this quality in our lives? How is this to be done?***

Before reading the next section, "Water: Sign of Life and Death" on page 32 of the text, have the group brainstorm all the connections that they make with the word *water.* Place these connections in two categories: positive connections and negative connections. Have the group read this section and then discuss:

- ***How is water both a sign of life and a sign of death?***

- ***Why is water a good symbol for the sacrament of Baptism?***

Have the group read about the New Rite of Baptism on page 32 of the text, and discuss:

- ***What is clearly stressed by the New Rite?***
- ***What are the main features of the New Rite?***

Summary

Present this question to the group: *Should a person be baptized as a child or as an adult?*

Ask each person in your group to write a brief essay, taking a position on the subject, and explaining why he or she chose that position. Several of the opposing points of view can then be read and discussed.

Section Nine
The Mass
Your Faith, pages 33-36

Synopsis

The Eucharist is the center of Christian life. It is the moment when we are most intimately united to each other and to God.

Materials Needed

- Paper and pens.
- Poster paper or newsprint.
- Felt-tipped pens.

Starting

Divide the group into smaller groups of six to eight persons. Each group is given one of the tasks below. Each task involves compiling a list and putting that list on a large piece of poster paper or newsprint. The tasks are:

(a) Compile a list of things whose meaning and value are unlimited.
(b) Compile a list of events that have changed the course of life on earth.
(c) Compile a list of ideas associated with strength and power.
(d) Compile a list of things that people center their lives around.
(e) Compile a list of things that add freshness to life.

Have each group share its list and allow members from other groups to add and/or discuss the items they see. Then discuss with the entire group:

- ***Is there any mention of religion and/or worship on any of the lists? Does it seem to be a predominant idea?***
- ***Do we usually associate such things as power, strength, value, etc. with religion or worship? Why is this the case?***
- ***Are the words* Eucharist *or* Mass *found on any of the lists?***

Sorting

Have the group read page 33 in the text and then discuss:

- ***Do our lists confirm or deny what is stated in the book about the Eucharist?***
- ***If we were to put all the information contained on our lists on one side of a scale and the Eucharist on the other side, would the scale be balanced or would it favor one side or the other? What does this indicate about the side that is favored?***
- ***What is meant by saying that the Mass has different aspects?***
- ***From a brief scan of the rest of the teaching about the Eucharist on pages 34-36, what are four major aspects of the Eucharist?***

Have the group read "This is the Word of the Lord" on page 34 of the text, and discuss:

- ***What does it mean to listen?***
- ***Is there anything to listen to at Mass?***
- ***What would Eucharist be without the Liturgy of the Word?***
- ***What does it mean to live by the Word of God?***
- ***What are the various parts of the Liturgy of the Word?***
- ***Why are these parts included in this section of the Mass?***

The second aspect of the Mass to be discussed is: offering in thanksgiving. Have your group read "We offer you in thanksgiving . . . " on page 34 of the text, and then discuss:

- ***What does it mean to thank?***
- ***What do we recall at each Eucharist celebration?***
- ***In what sense is the Eucharist an offering of thanks?***
- ***In what sense is the Eucharist a living sacrifice?***
- ***What is the connection between the Eucharist and the Exodus in the Old Testament?***
- ***Is this offering in the hands of the priest only?***

The third aspect of the Mass to be discussed is: being called to the Table of the Lord. Have your group read "Happy are those who are called . . ." on page 35 of the text, and then discuss:

- ***What does it mean to share a meal?***
- ***In what sense is the Mass a meal?***
- ***What are the various reasons someone might go to Mass?***
- ***Are you happy to be called to the Lord's supper?***
- ***Do you feel a personal call to the Table of the Lord?***
- ***What is the difference between saying "hearing Mass" and "celebrating the Eucharist"?***

The fourth aspect of the Mass to be discussed is the unity of gathering we experience in the Eucharist. Have your group read "Gather all who share . . ." on page 35 of the text, and then discuss:

- ***Is the Eucharist best described by saying it is a personal union with our Lord?***
- ***How is Christian love a necessary consequence of Holy Communion?***
- ***What is the significance of the words "Go, the Mass is ended"?***
- ***What can be done to make the Mass more of a community celebration?***

Have the group read "Christ is present in the Eucharist" on page 36 of the text, and then discuss:

- ***What does it mean to say Jesus is present in the Eucharist?***
- ***What does Jesus himself have to say about Eucharist?***
- ***What has been said about the Eucharist throughout the centuries? With which ideas do you agree most strongly?***

Summary

Present the following dialogue to your group and have them react, adding to it and discussing it.

Peter: Let's give up on these old rituals and come up with something new.

Ann: Giving up on the old isn't the answer. Let's look at the roots and sources of our present Eucharist and develop these into meaningful rituals for today.

Peter: Let's face it. The Eucharist seems to be something that is done for us and to us and that's the way it should be. It's all in the hands of the priest.

Ann: Eucharist means breaking bread together. It is something that should demand an active role for all present.

Peter: Eucharist and our lives are like water and oil. They just don't mix.

Ann: Now wait a minute! The only way Eucharist makes sense is if it in some way helps us live our lives as Christians.

Section Ten
The Sacrament of Forgiveness
Your Faith, pages 37-40

Synopsis

In the sacrament of Reconciliation, God reveals his unlimited forgiveness; for man's part, the sacrament is a call to conversion—a heartfelt desire to change.

Materials Needed

- Paper and pens.
- For this session, it would be ideal to have a priest demonstrate the New Rite and answer questions about it.

Starting

To develop the idea of reform/renewal as the center of the sacrament of Reconciliation, divide the group into groups of five and have each group develop a verbal portrait of a person their age who has gotten himself involved in a series of fairly serious problems—who, in a sense, has gotten lost or strayed away. Instruct them to leave the story open-ended so that other groups might suggest appropriate conclusions later on. When groups are finished, the stories should be shared and discussed as follows:

- ***If the person in the story were a friend of yours, would you be able to forgive him or her?***
- ***What would each person in each story have to do in order to "make things right" again?***
- ***Would he or she have to do more than confess?***
- ***Is there a difference between confessing and reforming?***
- ***In your view, which is closer to the real purpose of the sacrament of Penance, confessing or reforming? Why?***
- ***Check the attitudes on page 37 in the book. Which attitudes seem to be concerned with confessing? Which seem to be concerned with reforming?***
- ***What is the importance of the proper attitude toward God in the sacrament of Penance? toward the Church? toward oneself?***

Ask those in your group to circle the attitudes on page 37 of the text that are most characteristic of their own with respect to the sacrament of Penance. Then discuss the ones that the group seems most interested in.

Sorting

Two questions frequently asked in connection with the New Rite are: ***Why do we need a New Rite, and why or how is it new?*** Have the group read page 38 in the text, and then discuss:

- ***Why is there a need for a New Rite? Do you feel this need in your own life?***
- ***Has the fundamental teaching on this sacrament changed?***
- ***What does the use of the word* Reconciliation *indicate?***
- ***In ordinary human terms, what are some situations that need reconciliation?***
- ***How is sin viewed within the New Rite?***
- ***Make a list of things that could be possible sins. How is it true to say that each of these is not only a private action but one that also injures the entire Christian community?***

Have the group read "The Essential Parts . . ." on page 39 of the text, and then discuss:

- ***In order for the people in the stories to reform, what steps needed to be taken?***
- ***How are these steps related to the essential parts of the sacrament of Reconciliation?***
- ***What happens when this sacrament is treated like a thing?***
- ***What is contrition?***
- ***Why is it true that going to the sacrament demands careful preparation?***
- ***In what way is it possible for the confession part of this sacrament to be changed according to the penitent's needs?***
- ***What does satisfaction mean? Is this a human need to be filled after we have wronged someone?***
- ***What kinds of penances are suggested by the New Rite? Do you agree with this approach?***
- ***How does the New Rite describe absolution?***
- ***What view of God seems to be held by those who formulated the New Rite?***

At this point it would be ideal to have a priest available to demonstrate the practice of the New Rite, and perhaps to answer any questions those in your group might have. If a priest is not available, the section on the New Rite of Penance on page 40 of the text could be read, and the three forms of the New Rite discussed. Also to be discussed here are the qualities of the New Rite that group members like and don't like.

Have the group read "Preparation for the Sacrament of Penance" at the top of page 40 in the text. Divide the group into smaller groups of six to eight persons. Each group should make up a list of ten questions that people might use to examine themselves prior to the sacrament of Reconciliation. These questions can be called an Examination of Conscience. When all the groups have finished, share the questions and have others in the group react to and add to these lists.

Summary

Having looked at the New Rite, pose the following question:

- ***How could we make people in our parish more aware of the value and structure of the New Rite?***

After discussing this question, divide the group into smaller groups of five and have each group produce a two-minute radio spot that says something about the New Rite for those who have had little or no contact with it as yet.

Section Eleven
The Sacrament of Orders
Your Faith, pages 41-44

Synopsis

The words of the bishop to the congregation and to the candidates at an ordination ceremony are an answer to the question "What is a priest?"

Materials Needed

- Paper and pens.

Starting

Present the following situation to your group:

- ***You are a priest who has just been given a brand new parish and told that you are in complete control of what happens in this parish for the next five years. The parish owns a church, a school building, a convent, and a rectory, as well as a parking lot and playing field. At present, the parish is slightly in debt and is situated in a middle-class neighborhood.***

Have your group consider this profile and let them add to it if they wish. Then have each person do the following individually:

- list their goals as priest for the next five years;
- list the things that need to be done in this setting during the course of the next five years, and the extent of their involvement in these activities.

After everyone has developed these lists, divide the class into groups to discuss their lists. From these discussions each group should develop a description of what it means to be a priest. These descriptions could be shared with the entire group and then discussed in terms of their own experience with the priesthood.

Sorting

The content for this section is taken directly from the bishop's remarks to the congregation and to the candidates to be ordained. Have your group read page 41 in the text which is the bishop's remarks to the congregation. Discuss:

- *Why is there a need for the People of God to consider carefully the position in the Church which the priest will have?*
- *As a layman, what is your reaction to the second paragraph of the bishop's remarks?*
- *What are the functions of priest as described in the third paragraph?*
- *What do you consider the most important line in this selection?*
- *If you were addressing the congregation at this kind of celebration, how would your remarks to them be different? If so, what would you say?*

Have one person in the group read aloud the paragraphs found on pages 42-44 in the text: "Then the Bishop Speaks to the Men Who Are to Be Ordained . . . ." Ask the rest of the group to listen as though they were candidates for ordination. Discuss:

- *What was going through your mind as you listened to this reading? What were your feelings?*
- *Pick out all the action words contained in this selection. What do they say about what it means to be a priest?*
- *What three-fold function of belief is mentioned in paragraph one?*
- *What does it mean to say, "Let the impact of your lives please the followers of Christ"? Is this possible or impossible to do?*
- *Why does the major portion of this statement deal with the celebration of the sacraments?*
- *What does the bishop say about the administering of each of the sacraments?*
- *What image is used at the end? What other contemporary images of the priesthood can you mention?*
- *How does the bishop's statement compare to your own plan of action (the one you planned earlier in this session) as a priest?*
- *What is the tone of this statement? Does it seem consistent with the sort of life style a priest is expected to lead?*

The bishop's remarks raise the question of practicality. At this point it would be valuable to have a priest react to the bishop's statement. If this is not possible, have people in your group work in smaller groups to reconstruct what they would see as a typical day in the life of a priest and create the situations that they think he would be likely to come into contact with. The following is offered as a starting point or guide:

- Sam asks: "You say I'm supposed to love my neighbor. There are eight million people in this city. Which ones are my neighbors?"
- Mary is considering leaving the Catholic Faith and becoming a Buddhist. She wants to know if there's really that much difference between the two religions.
- A young man and a young girl come in hand-in-hand. They say they met last week and it was love at first sight. They would like to arrange for a wedding one month from today.

Two issues that could be mentioned and/or discussed at this point would be (a) a married priesthood and (b) women as priests. If time permits, perhaps those in your group could write pro/con position papers on each of these topics, to be discussed in the group.

Summary

Divide the group into smaller groups to do one of the following:

- Write a job description for a priest.
- Plan a TV program that would be aimed at getting young people interested in the work of the priesthood.

Section Twelve
Confirmation and Sacrament of the Sick
Your Faith, **pages 45-48**

Synopsis

The sacrament of Confirmation is a sacrament of strength and maturity — of the Spirit bringing to a fullness all that God's love can mean in our lives. The sacrament of the sick is also about restoration to fullness; it demonstrates God's concern with the bodily and spiritual strengths of the sick and dying.

Materials Needed

- Chalkboard and chalk, or newsprint and a felt-tipped pen.
- Paper and pens.

Starting

Have the group brainstorm the possible uses of and connections between the word *strength* and the word *power.* List the types of strength, (moral, physical, social, etc.) on the chalkboard or on newsprint. Divide the group into smaller groups of six to eight persons. Each group should take a different meaning of the word *strength* and illustrate it either by drawing a comic strip or planning and performing a comedy skit. These should be shared and then discussed as follows:

- ***Does the word* strength *have more than one meaning? What are some of these meanings?***
- ***Under what circumstances would you call someone "strong"?***
- ***How would you test someone for spiritual strength? for physical strength? for strength of character?***
- ***Are there situations where apparent weakness is actually a sign of strength (e.g., backing away from an unnecessary right)?***

Ask the group to read page 45 in the text, then discuss:

- ***What type of strength or power did the apostles receive on Pentecost? What was their power source?***
- ***Is this source what you usually associate with strength?***

- ***Describe a particular strength you would like to possess.***

Sorting

The text deals with two sacraments in this section: Confirmation and Anointing — the sacrament of the sick. Both are in some way connected to the idea of strength.

Have the group read "How Could Others Receive the Spirit?" and "Strengthened in the Spirit" on page 46 of the text. Then discuss:

- ***When does a person first receive the Spirit? (It is a common misconception that a person first receives the Spirit at Confirmation. That is incorrect. The Church teaches that a person receives the Spirit when baptized.)***
- ***What is the significance of the imposition of hands?***
- ***What is the significance of the anointing?***
- ***What does the word*** **confirmation** ***mean?***
- ***What kind of strength does the Christian receive in the sacrament of Confirmation?***
- ***How is Confirmation a completion of Baptism?***
- ***What is included in the celebration of the sacrament of Confirmation to show its connection to Baptism?***
- ***What is meant by spiritual maturity?***

Before reading the next section, have small groups make an inventory of possible gifts/talents that exist in people in the world today and then discuss the question of how these talents/gifts could be used in situations that need healing. Have each group share the result of its work. Then have the group read "To Renew the Face of the Earth" on page 46 of the text, and discuss:

- ***"To renew the face of the earth" – is this a powerful thought? Why?***
- ***What sensitivities and responsibilities does maturity bring with it?***
- ***Why is Confirmation called the sacrament of social action?***
- ***What are some social action issues from your list above?***
- ***What strengths are needed to heal these social problems?***
- ***Are there any social action projects that arise out of your own local circumstances?***
- ***Why are these talents/gifts sometimes not used?***
- ***How would you answer someone who said: "I have no special talents or gifts"?***

Have your group read the listing and description of the gifts of the Holy Spirit on page 47 of the text. Then discuss:

- ***What gifts are celebrated at the sacrament of Confirmation?***
- ***Do we receive these gifts automatically?***
- ***Which do you feel are needed the most?***

In moving on to the second portion of this section, it is important to note that both the sacrament of Confirmation and the sacrament of the sick use the anointing of oil as a major symbolic gesture within their respective rituals. Oil is a symbol of strength, but is has lost this meaning in our contemporary society.

Have your group read "The Sacrament of the Sick" on pages 47-48 of the text, and then discuss:

- ***What is the emphasis in the sacrament of the sick – spiritual or physical?***
- ***Is this sacrament of any help to a person who is fearful of sickness and death?***
- ***When should this sacrament be received?***
- ***What kind of strength does this sacrament provide?***
- ***What is said in the directives for the New Rite about old age? about children?***
- ***How is this sacrament administered?***

Summary

The stress in this section has been on the idea of strength, both for the healthy and for the sick. A way to conclude would be to have your group discuss the following:

- ***What would be a test of strength that you could give to a Christian?***

Section Thirteen
Mary, Mother of All Christians
Your Faith, pages 49-52

Synopsis

Mary is the person God chose to give his Son humanity. Mary's response to God is the perfect model of the Christian's response to God in faith.

Materials Needed

- Paper and pens.

Starting

Present the following situation to your group:

- ***This Friday evening during prime time, the major TV networks will each present a contest event that centers on women. One network will present the "Ms. Feminity Contest." A second network will air the "Ms. Christian Women Contest." The third will be the "Mother of the World Contest." You are all judges for one of these contests.***

Divide the class into three groups (or double up on assignments and divide into six groups). Each group is a panel of judges in one of the three contests listed above. Their tasks are:

(a) to determine the criteria they would apply in selecting a winner for their contest and listing these qualities/criteria;

(b) to describe the concept of womanhood that is likely to be in the minds of those who sponsor these contests.

When all groups have completed their work, have each group present the results of its work to the rest of the groups and allow for feedback and comparisons to be made. Then discuss:

- ***How did you feel as you were drawing up the criteria by which another person would be judged?***
- ***Which of the three shows do you think would get the most viewers? What does that say about our contemporary viewpoint of women?***

- ***Which of the shows would women's lib persons be least likely to watch? Why?***
- ***Which of the shows would be most likely viewed by adolescents?***
- ***Which of the shows would you yourself be most interested in? Why?***

Have your group scan through the section and try to pick out qualities associated with Mary. Then discuss:

- ***What are the qualities of Mary that are mentioned in this section?***
- ***Which TV contest would be closest to the qualities of Mary mentioned in this section?***
- ***Would Mary be a winner on any of these shows?***

Sorting

Before proceeding any further, ask your group to reflect on their past understanding of Mary and how they view Mary right now. Ask each person to write a brief statement of where he or she is with respect to Mary as one of the more important aspects of the Catholic Faith. These statements could be shared.

Next, ask your group to read pages 49-50 in the text. Then discuss:

- ***Why is Mary the greatest of all mothers?***
- ***In giving Jesus his humanity, what of herself did she pass on to him?***
- ***How is Mary central to Catholic thinking about the Incarnation?***
- ***What would our faith be like if it did not include some statement about Mary's place?***
- ***In saying "yes" to God, how is Mary a model for people in the Church?***
- ***In thinking about Mary and the Church together, how is our view of the Church a healthier one?***
- ***What do you think is the extent of devotion to Mary today?***
- ***What does it mean to imitate the attitude of Mary?***

Have your group read "The Attentive Virgin" and then discuss:

- ***What does attentiveness mean?***
- ***To whom was Mary attentive?***
- ***What are the three moments from Scripture where Mary's attentiveness is most clear?***
- ***How does attentiveness also demand courage?***

- ***What is the value of being attentive to the Word of God in our own lives?***
- ***What is the value of cultivating our faith as Mary did?***
- ***How did Mary achieve maturity? What did she gain as a result of striving for maturity?***
- ***Since Mary responded so well to the word of God, in what way does she embody what might be called the "feminine side" of God?***

Have the group read "The Virgin in Prayer" on page 51 of the text. Then discuss:

- ***How is the title "virgin in prayer" applicable to Mary? to the Church?***
- ***What is meant by "placing oneself in the presence of Christ"?***

This would be a good place to survey attitudes and practices toward prayer. In this regard the following questions might be of help:

- ***Do you pray privately?***
- ***How would you describe your attitude toward your own spiritual life?***
- ***What do you think of people who pray?***
- ***Did you ever pray for something or for someone and feel that you received an answer to your prayer?***
- ***Do you have a definite time and place for prayer?***
- ***Have you ever kept a prayer journal?***
- ***In what situations are you most likely to pray?***
- ***Would you rather pray alone or in a group?***
- ***Do you think that God answers prayers in more than one way?***
- ***Do you pray even when you feel doubtful and full of disbelief?***

Have the group read "The Virgin Mother" on page 52 of the text, and discuss:

- ***What was the controversy surrounding the humanity/divinity of Jesus?***
- ***What is the symbolism of Mary's virginity?***

Summary

In reflecting on whether Mary is a contemporary and living model for Christians today, you could discuss the following three questions:

- ***Do we know suffering and loneliness?***
- ***Have we experienced rejection and exile of various sorts?***
- ***Are we sometimes confused by what we perceive as God's plan for us?***

Section Fourteen
Christian Marriage
Your Faith, pages 53-56

Synopsis

The sacrament of Matrimony enables a married couple to experience a bond of love between them and to be a sign of Jesus' love through ordinary human relationship.

Materials Needed

- Paper and pens.

Starting

Pose the following two questions for reflection:

- ***What makes a marriage a rich and rewarding experience?***
- ***What makes a marriage a sour and sad experience?***

Divide the group into smaller groups of four to six persons. Each group should discuss the two questions above and then develop a brief skit that illustrates an answer to the question: *What is it like to be married?*

Each group should present its skit. Then the experience can be discussed as follows:

- ***Which skit seemed to be most realistic?***
- ***Do these skits seem to give marriage a good press or a bad press?***
- ***What were the attitudes that seemed to make marriage a rich and rewarding experience?***
- ***What were the attitudes that seemed to make marriage a sad and sour experience?***
- ***What seems to be the greatest obstacle to a good marriage?***
- ***What misconceptions about married life did the skits point out?***
- ***Is marriage a thing of the past?***
- ***If marriage were suddenly outlawed, what effect would this have upon society? upon you?***

Sorting

Have the group read page 53 in the text. Discuss as follows:

- ***Does the Church's position on marriage seem optimistic or pessimistic?***
- ***What are the incorrect ways of viewing marriage?***
- ***Would society do better without traditional forms of marriage?***
- ***What's the difference between a civil marriage and a Christian marriage?***
- ***Did the Church initiate the institution of marriage?***
- ***What does a "Christianized" marriage do for the married couple?***
- ***What does it do for the Church?***
- ***Did any of the skits show anything of the spiritual dimension of marriage?***

At this point the text shifts the discussion to the idea of love. Before reading the next few parts, have the group consider the following:

- ***How would you describe love to someone who never heard the word?***
- ***Are any of the skits appropriate to describe the nature of love?***

Have the group read "A Bond of Love" and "A Sign of Christ's Love" on page 54 and "Marriage: A Sacrament" on page 55 of the text. Then discuss:

- ***Where is love derived from?***
- ***How is God's love described?***
- ***Is it enough to know the love of God?***
- ***What is the nature of Christian love?***
- ***What is the nature of Christian married love?***
- ***In what way is marriage a sacrament?***
- ***"To love one another is to wish for one another eternal life with God and to lead one another to it." Does this "say it all" about Christian marriage?***

Have the group read "The Love Relationship: What Scripture Tells Us" on page 54 of the text. Then discuss:

- ***What does the Old Testament Book of Hosea say about marriage?***
- ***What does the New Testament say about love?***
- ***What is St. John's reflection on love for the early Christian community?***

Before reading the next part, "The Everyday Life of Marriage: A School of Love," on page 55 of the text, have the group share ideas about the day-to-day experience of marriage as portrayed in their skits and from their own experience. Then ask them to read the section and discuss:

- ***What is the significance of the idea of marriage as a school of love?***
- ***Why is it difficult to see that husbands and wives make Jesus present to one another?***
- ***Where and when do married couples make Jesus present?***
- ***How is "making love" a good description of sexual intercourse?***
- ***Can extramarital or premarital sexual relationships be a true expression of love?***
- ***Does love grow and express itself in other ways besides the sex act?***
- ***In what way are arguments and disagreements expressions of love?***
- ***Why are St. Paul's words about love significant for the married couple?***
- ***According to this section in the book, what is the key to a successful marriage?***

Present the following situation to your group.

- ***Imagine you are a parent of a teen-age son or daughter who is involved in the following activities: (a) drug abuse; (b) alcohol abuse; (c) shoplifting; (d) nonattendance at Mass; (e) wants to drop out of high school; (f) is sexually promiscuous.***

Ask those in your group to rank these problems according to which one would bother them the most, the second most, etc. Discuss their rankings and how they might go about handling the situation.

Have the group read page 56 in the text. Then discuss:

- ***Does a marriage have to be child-bearing in order to carry on God's creative love?***
- ***How are parents the first teachers of their children?***
- ***What is important to teach a young child? A teen-ager?***
- ***Is Christianity caught, or is it taught?***
- ***As a parent, which quality in children bothers you the most?***
- ***As a young person, which quality in parents bothers you the most?***

Summary

Have the group rank the following reasons for getting married according to what they feel is the most valid, second most valid, etc.

(a) having a sexual partner;

(b) having and raising kids;

(c) having someone to be with so you won't be alone;

(d) forming an economic partnership;

(e) having fun together;

(f) knowing that one person understands you better than anyone else in the world.

Discuss the group's rankings and formulate conclusions as to how these reasons coincide (or do not coincide) with the characteristics of married love on page 56 of the text.

Section Fifteen
Christ Will Come Again
Your Faith, pages 57-60

Synopsis

Our life in Jesus Christ is a source of meaning and hope as we face the suffering of this world and the uncertainties of the next.

Materials Needed

- Paper and pens.

Starting

Involve your group in a silent reflection period in which they consider the following questions:

- How would you like to see the world end?
- What would you like eternity to be?

Allow some time for a *written* reflection on these two questions. Then ask for a sharing and discussion of them.

Ask the group to read page 57 in the text. Then discuss:

- ***Did you find the written reflection difficult?***
- ***How would you like to see the world end?***
- ***What do you think most people think of what they consider the end of the world?***
- ***How does the unbeliever's view of the end of the world differ from the believer's view?***
- ***What accounts for this difference?***
- ***What does belief in the Resurrection do for the Christian's belief in the end of the world?***
- ***How did the early Christian community express their view of the end of the world?***

Sorting

Have your group read "The Last Judgment" on page 58 of the text and then discuss:

- ***What do you think of when you think of the word* judgment?**
- ***On what is our judgment based?***

- ***What are some of the activities of one who would seek to be a part of the kingdom of God?***
- ***How would you summarize this teaching about the Last Judgment?***
- ***Do we judge ourselves or does God judge us?***
- ***How does the prophet Isaiah describe the end of the world?***
- ***How does the Eucharistic Prayer describe the end of the world?***

Have the group read "The Death of a Christian" on pages 58-59 of the text. Then discuss:

- ***What one word describes how you feel toward your own death?***
- ***What one word describes how you feel toward the death of others?***
- ***Does the believer have any consolation with respect to death?***
- ***Did God intend man to die?***
- ***How did death become a part of the human condition?***
- ***What did Jesus do to death?***
- ***J.R.R. Tolkien writes in*** **The Fellowship of the Rings:** ***"Still around the corner there may wait a new road or a secret gate." Does this quote have any application to the Christian viewpoint on death?***
- ***If you could imagine death as another person and you were able to speak to it, what question would you ask it?***

Have the group read "The Communion of Saints" on page 59 of the text and then discuss:

- ***What are some words that come to your mind when you think of the word saint?***
- ***How does St. Paul describe a saint?***
- ***What is the value of being in touch with the lives of the saints?***
- ***Why does the Church keep the saints before our eyes?***

Have the group read "Our Life in Christ" on page 60 of the text and then discuss:

- ***How is the history of the Church a history of growth?***
- ***What is the image that Jesus used to describe the kingdom of God?***
- ***Are there other contemporary images that might be used to describe the kingdom of God in this way?***
- ***What would be the result if we, as Christians, failed to grow?***
- ***What does St. Paul mean when he says to put on Jesus Christ?***

- ***How is this done on a day-to-day basis?***
- ***Is the growth in love of Christ primarily our task or God's?***
- ***What is our part in this process?***
- ***What is the meaning of the Eucharist with respect to putting on Jesus Christ?***

Summary

Ask those in the group to look at the description of the end of the world and eternity which they wrote at the start of this session. Discuss points of comparison between their reflections and the reflections offered in this section. Also discuss the following:

- ***When thinking about death, the end of the world, and eternity, how do the believer's thoughts differ from the unbeliever's thoughts?***

For a Closing Session

This session is meant to be a review of what has gone before as well as a catalyst for further study.

Ask each person to jot down 10 things that he or she would like to possess. Divide into smaller groups and have each small group list the 10 most important or common possessions on a piece of newsprint. Taking each item one by one, have each group discuss and note a way of fulfilling that particular need in their life. When all the groups have finished, have them share their newsprint charts with the other groups. Then discuss:

- ***What is the role of Jesus in your fulfilling or possessing the above items?***
- ***Has the program* Your Faith *enabled you to see what you want to possess in a clearer way?***
- ***Has* Your Faith *increased your faith?***
- ***Could Jesus and faith in him be of any help in attaining any of the things you want to possess?***

Based on what has been experienced in this program, ask each person to write up a statement of his own personal creed. After these have been shared, ask:

- ***Do the ideas in your creed reflect any ideas from* Your Faith?**
- ***If you could put only one "item" from this program into your creed, what would that one item be?***
- ***What questions has this program raised in your mind?***

Cinema Suggestions

From time to time a film may offer refreshing possibilities for creative reflection and discussion. The following films have been selected to correlate to a theme in each of the sections of **Your Faith.** (The question listed after each film is an attempt to focus on the theme in that particular section.) It is suggested that you order a film a month in advance and preview it yourself before showing it to your group.

Section 1	Jesus Is the Center of Our Faith Film: ***Epiphania*** (Teleketics) Question: Who is Jesus?
Section 2	Background to the Life of Jesus Film: ***The Man From Inner Space*** (Paulist) Question: Was Jesus an unexpected Messiah?
Section 3	Jesus Revealed God to Man Film: The Stray (Teleketics) Question: What kind of God did Jesus reveal?
Section 4	Jesus Is Our Redeemer Film: ***Jesus, B.C.*** (Paulist) Question: Why did Jesus come?
Section 5	Jesus Sends the Holy Spirit Film: ***Turned Round to See*** (Teleketics) Question: What happens when the Spirit touches our life?
Section 6	The Church Makes Jesus Present Today Film: ***Parable*** (Viewfinders) Question: What is the ministry of the Church?
Section 7	The New Testament Film: ***Love to Kill*** (Learning Corporation) Question: Does the essential Gospel message change?
Section 8	The Sacraments — Baptism Film: ***Skating Rink*** (Learning Corporation) Question: How does it feel to be accepted and to belong?

Section 9 — The Mass
Film: ***Mark of the Clown*** (Mass Media Ministries)
Question: What is the nature of Christian worship?

Section 10 — The Sacrament of Forgiveness
Film: ***Prodigal Father*** (Paulist)
Question: What is the forgiveness of the kingdom of God?

Section 11 — The Sacrament of Orders
Film: ***Dancing Prophet*** (Teleketics)
Question: What is essential to ministry to the People of God?

Section 12 — Confirmation and the Sacrament of the Sick
Film: ***Bill Cosby on Prejudice*** (Pyramid)
Question: What are the social issues that face us today?

Section 13 — Mary, Mother of All Christians
Film: ***Crystal Lee Jordan*** (Indiana University)
Question: What is the nature of contemporary Christian personhood?

Section 14 — Christian Marriage
Film: ***Where Were You at the Battle of the Bulge, Kid?*** (Paulist)
Question: How does the married couple make Jesus present to each other and to their children?

Section 15 — Christ Will Come Again
Film: ***Where All Things Belong*** (Essentia)
Question: How do we experience resurrection?

Film Distributors

Essentia
P.O. Box 129
Tiburon, CA 94920

Indiana University
AudioVisual Center
Bloomington, IN 47401

Paulist Productions
P.O. Box 1057
Pacific Palisades, CA 90272

Pyramid Films
P.O. Box 1048
Santa Monica, CA 90406

Learning Corporation of America
1350 Avenue of the Americas
New York, New York 10019

Mass Media Ministries
2116 N. Charles Street
Baltimore, Maryland 21218

TeleKETICS
1229 South Santee Street
Los Angeles, CA 90015

ViewFinders, Inc.
2550 Green Bay Road
Evanston, IL 60204